My Lineage

1st Generation

Me:
Date of Birth:
Place of Birth:
Siblings:

Places of Residence:

Date of Death:
Place of Death:

Other Information:

My Mother's Side

2nd Generation

My Mother:
Date of Birth:
Place of Birth:
Siblings:

Places of Residence:

Date of Death:
Place of Death:

Other Information:

Resources:

My Maternal Grandmother:

Date of Birth:

Place of Birth:

Siblings:

Places of Residence:

Date of Death:

Place of Death:

Other Information:

Resources:

∞∞∞∞∞∞∞∞∞∞∞∞∞∞

My Maternal Grandfather:

Date of Birth:

Place of Birth:

Siblings:

Places of Residence:

Date of Death:

Place of Death:

Other Information:

Resources:

4th Generation – Daughter's Name:

My Maternal Great Grandmother:

Date of Birth:

Place of Birth:

Siblings:

Places of Residence:

Date of Death:

Place of Death:

Other Information:

Resources:

∞∞∞∞∞∞∞∞∞∞∞∞∞

My Maternal Great Grandfather:

Date of Birth:

Place of Birth:

Siblings:

Places of Residence:

Date of Death:

Place of Death:

Other Information:

Resources:

4th Generation – Son's Name:

My Maternal Great Grandmother:
Date of Birth:
Place of Birth:
Siblings:

Places of Residence:

Date of Death:
Place of Death:

Other Information:

Resources:

∞∞∞∞∞∞∞∞∞∞∞∞∞

My Maternal Great Grandfather:
Date of Birth:
Place of Birth:
Siblings:

Places of Residence:

Date of Death:
Place of Death:

Other Information:

Resources:

5th Generation – Daughter's Name:

My Maternal Great Great Grandmother:
Date of Birth:
Place of Birth:
Siblings:

Places of Residence:

Date of Death:
Place of Death:

Other Information:

Resources:

∞∞∞∞∞∞∞∞∞∞∞∞∞∞

My Maternal Great Great Grandfather:
Date of Birth:
Place of Birth:
Siblings:

Places of Residence:

Date of Death:
Place of Death:

Other Information:

Resources:

My Maternal Great Great Grandmother:

Date of Birth:

Place of Birth:

Siblings:

Places of Residence:

Date of Death:

Place of Death:

Other Information:

Resources:

∞∞∞∞∞∞∞∞∞∞∞∞∞∞

My Maternal Great Great Grandfather:

Date of Birth:

Place of Birth:

Siblings:

Places of Residence:

Date of Death:

Place of Death:

Other Information:

Resources:

My Maternal Great Great Grandmother:

Date of Birth:

Place of Birth:

Siblings:

Places of Residence:

Date of Death:

Place of Death:

Other Information:

Resources:

∞∞∞∞∞∞∞∞∞∞∞∞∞∞

My Maternal Great Great Grandfather:

Date of Birth:

Place of Birth:

Siblings:

Places of Residence:

Date of Death:

Place of Death:

Other Information:

Resources:

5th Generation – Son's Name:

My Maternal Great Great Grandmother:
Date of Birth:
Place of Birth:
Siblings:

Places of Residence:

Date of Death:
Place of Death:

Other Information:

Resources:

∞∞∞∞∞∞∞∞∞∞∞∞∞

My Maternal Great Great Grandfather:
Date of Birth:
Place of Birth:
Siblings:

Places of Residence:

Date of Death:
Place of Death:

Other Information:

Resources:

6th Generation – Daughter's Name:

My Maternal Great Great Great Grandmother:

Date of Birth:

Place of Birth:

Siblings:

Places of Residence:

Date of Death:

Place of Death:

Other Information:

Resources:

∞∞∞∞∞∞∞∞∞∞∞∞∞

My Maternal Great Great Great Grandfather:

Date of Birth:

Place of Birth:

Siblings:

Places of Residence:

Date of Death:

Place of Death:

Other Information:

Resources:

6th Generation – Son's Name:

My Maternal Great Great Great Grandmother:
Date of Birth:
Place of Birth:
Siblings:

Places of Residence:

Date of Death:
Place of Death:

Other Information:

Resources:

∞∞∞∞∞∞∞∞∞∞∞∞∞

My Maternal Great Great Great Grandfather:
Date of Birth:
Place of Birth:
Siblings:

Places of Residence:

Date of Death:
Place of Death:

Other Information:

Resources:

6th Generation – Daughter's Name:

My Maternal Great Great Great Grandmother:
Date of Birth:
Place of Birth:
Siblings:

Places of Residence:

Date of Death:
Place of Death:

Other Information:

Resources:

∞∞∞∞∞∞∞∞∞∞∞∞∞

My Maternal Great Great Great Grandfather:
Date of Birth:
Place of Birth:
Siblings:

Places of Residence:

Date of Death:
Place of Death:

Other Information:

Resources:

6ᵗʰ Generation – Son's Name:

My Maternal Great Great Great Grandmother:
Date of Birth:
Place of Birth:
Siblings:

Places of Residence:

Date of Death:
Place of Death:

Other Information:

Resources:

∞∞∞∞∞∞∞∞∞∞∞∞∞∞

My Maternal Great Great Great Grandfather:
Date of Birth:
Place of Birth:
Siblings:

Places of Residence:

Date of Death:
Place of Death:

Other Information:

Resources:

My Maternal Great Great Great Grandmother:

Date of Birth:

Place of Birth:

Siblings:

Places of Residence:

Date of Death:

Place of Death:

Other Information:

Resources:

∞∞∞∞∞∞∞∞∞∞∞∞∞∞

My Maternal Great Great Great Grandfather:

Date of Birth:

Place of Birth:

Siblings:

Places of Residence:

Date of Death:

Place of Death:

Other Information:

Resources:

6ᵗʰ Generation – Son's Name:

My Maternal Great Great Great Grandmother:

Date of Birth:

Place of Birth:

Siblings:

Places of Residence:

Date of Death:

Place of Death:

Other Information:

Resources:

∞∞∞∞∞∞∞∞∞∞∞∞∞∞

My Maternal Great Great Great Grandfather:

Date of Birth:

Place of Birth:

Siblings:

Places of Residence:

Date of Death:

Place of Death:

Other Information:

Resources:

6th Generation – Daughter's Name:

My Maternal Great Great Great Grandmother:

Date of Birth:

Place of Birth:

Siblings:

Places of Residence:

Date of Death:

Place of Death:

Other Information:

Resources:

∞∞∞∞∞∞∞∞∞∞∞∞∞∞

My Maternal Great Great Great Grandfather:

Date of Birth:

Place of Birth:

Siblings:

Places of Residence:

Date of Death:

Place of Death:

Other Information:

Resources:

6th Generation – Son's Name:

My Maternal Great Great Great Grandmother:

Date of Birth:

Place of Birth:

Siblings:

Places of Residence:

Date of Death:

Place of Death:

Other Information:

Resources:

∞∞∞∞∞∞∞∞∞∞∞∞∞

My Maternal Great Great Great Grandfather:

Date of Birth:

Place of Birth:

Siblings:

Places of Residence:

Date of Death:

Place of Death:

Other Information:

Resources:

7th Generation – Daughter's Name:

My Maternal Great Great Great Great Grandmother:

Date of Birth:

Place of Birth:

Siblings:

Places of Residence:

Date of Death:

Place of Death:

Other Information:

Resources:

∞∞∞∞∞∞∞∞∞∞∞∞∞∞

My Maternal Great Great Great Great Grandfather:

Date of Birth:

Place of Birth:

Siblings:

Places of Residence:

Date of Death:

Place of Death:

Other Information:

Resources:

7ᵗʰ Generation – Son's Name:

My Maternal Great Great Great Great Grandmother:
Date of Birth:
Place of Birth:
Siblings:

Places of Residence:

Date of Death:
Place of Death:

Other Information:

Resources:

∞∞∞∞∞∞∞∞∞∞∞∞∞∞∞

My Maternal Great Great Great Great Grandfather:
Date of Birth:
Place of Birth:
Siblings:

Places of Residence:

Date of Death:
Place of Death:

Other Information:

Resources:

My Maternal Great Great Great Great Grandmother:

Date of Birth:

Place of Birth:

Siblings:

Places of Residence:

Date of Death:

Place of Death:

Other Information:

Resources:

∞∞∞∞∞∞∞∞∞∞∞∞∞

My Maternal Great Great Great Great Grandfather:

Date of Birth:

Place of Birth:

Siblings:

Places of Residence:

Date of Death:

Place of Death:

Other Information:

Resources:

7th Generation – Son's Name:

My Maternal Great Great Great Great Grandmother:
Date of Birth:
Place of Birth:
Siblings:

Places of Residence:

Date of Death:
Place of Death:

Other Information:

Resources:

∞∞∞∞∞∞∞∞∞∞∞∞∞

My Maternal Great Great Great Great Grandfather:
Date of Birth:
Place of Birth:
Siblings:

Places of Residence:

Date of Death:
Place of Death:

Other Information:

Resources:

7th Generation – Daughter's Name:

My Maternal Great Great Great Great Grandmother:

Date of Birth:

Place of Birth:

Siblings:

Places of Residence:

Date of Death:

Place of Death:

Other Information:

Resources:

∞∞∞∞∞∞∞∞∞∞∞∞∞

My Maternal Great Great Great Great Grandfather:

Date of Birth:

Place of Birth:

Siblings:

Places of Residence:

Date of Death:

Place of Death:

Other Information:

Resources:

My Maternal Great Great Great Great Grandmother:

Date of Birth:

Place of Birth:

Siblings:

Places of Residence:

Date of Death:

Place of Death:

Other Information:

Resources:

∞∞∞∞∞∞∞∞∞∞∞∞∞∞∞

My Maternal Great Great Great Great Grandfather:

Date of Birth:

Place of Birth:

Siblings:

Places of Residence:

Date of Death:

Place of Death:

Other Information:

Resources:

My Maternal Great Great Great Great Grandmother:

Date of Birth:

Place of Birth:

Siblings:

Places of Residence:

Date of Death:

Place of Death:

Other Information:

Resources:

∞∞∞∞∞∞∞∞∞∞∞∞∞∞

My Maternal Great Great Great Great Grandfather:

Date of Birth:

Place of Birth:

Siblings:

Places of Residence:

Date of Death:

Place of Death:

Other Information:

Resources:

7th Generation – Son's Name:

My Maternal Great Great Great Great Grandmother:

Date of Birth:

Place of Birth:

Siblings:

Places of Residence:

Date of Death:

Place of Death:

Other Information:

Resources:

∞∞∞∞∞∞∞∞∞∞∞∞∞

My Maternal Great Great Great Great Grandfather:

Date of Birth:

Place of Birth:

Siblings:

Places of Residence:

Date of Death:

Place of Death:

Other Information:

Resources:

7th Generation – Daughter's Name:

My Maternal Great Great Great Great Grandmother:
Date of Birth:
Place of Birth:
Siblings:

Places of Residence:

Date of Death:
Place of Death:

Other Information:

Resources:

∞∞∞∞∞∞∞∞∞∞∞∞∞

My Maternal Great Great Great Great Grandfather:
Date of Birth:
Place of Birth:
Siblings:

Places of Residence:

Date of Death:
Place of Death:

Other Information:

Resources:

My Maternal Great Great Great Great Grandmother:

Date of Birth:

Place of Birth:

Siblings:

Places of Residence:

Date of Death:

Place of Death:

Other Information:

Resources:

∞∞∞∞∞∞∞∞∞∞∞∞∞∞

My Maternal Great Great Great Great Grandfather:

Date of Birth:

Place of Birth:

Siblings:

Places of Residence:

Date of Death:

Place of Death:

Other Information:

Resources:

My Maternal Great Great Great Great Grandmother:
Date of Birth:
Place of Birth:
Siblings:

Places of Residence:

Date of Death:
Place of Death:

Other Information:

Resources:

∞∞∞∞∞∞∞∞∞∞∞∞∞

My Maternal Great Great Great Great Grandfather:
Date of Birth:
Place of Birth:
Siblings:

Places of Residence:

Date of Death:
Place of Death:

Other Information:

Resources:

7th Generation – Son's Name:

My Maternal Great Great Great Great Grandmother:
Date of Birth:
Place of Birth:
Siblings:

Places of Residence:

Date of Death:
Place of Death:

Other Information:

Resources:

∞∞∞∞∞∞∞∞∞∞∞∞∞∞

My Maternal Great Great Great Great Grandfather:
Date of Birth:
Place of Birth:
Siblings:

Places of Residence:

Date of Death:
Place of Death:

Other Information:

Resources:

My Maternal Great Great Great Great Grandmother:

Date of Birth:

Place of Birth:

Siblings:

Places of Residence:

Date of Death:

Place of Death:

Other Information:

Resources:

∞∞∞∞∞∞∞∞∞∞∞∞∞∞

My Maternal Great Great Great Great Grandfather:

Date of Birth:

Place of Birth:

Siblings:

Places of Residence:

Date of Death:

Place of Death:

Other Information:

Resources:

7th Generation – Son's Name:

My Maternal Great Great Great Great Grandmother:

Date of Birth:

Place of Birth:

Siblings:

Places of Residence:

Date of Death:

Place of Death:

Other Information:

Resources:

∞∞∞∞∞∞∞∞∞∞∞∞∞

My Maternal Great Great Great Great Grandfather:

Date of Birth:

Place of Birth:

Siblings:

Places of Residence:

Date of Death:

Place of Death:

Other Information:

Resources:

My Maternal Great Great Great Great Grandmother:

Date of Birth:

Place of Birth:

Siblings:

Places of Residence:

Date of Death:

Place of Death:

Other Information:

Resources:

∞∞∞∞∞∞∞∞∞∞∞∞∞

My Maternal Great Great Great Great Grandfather:

Date of Birth:

Place of Birth:

Siblings:

Places of Residence:

Date of Death:

Place of Death:

Other Information:

Resources:

7th Generation – Son's Name:

My Maternal Great Great Great Great Grandmother:

Date of Birth:

Place of Birth:

Siblings:

Places of Residence:

Date of Death:

Place of Death:

Other Information:

Resources:

∞∞∞∞∞∞∞∞∞∞∞∞∞

My Maternal Great Great Great Great Grandfather:

Date of Birth:

Place of Birth:

Siblings:

Places of Residence:

Date of Death:

Place of Death:

Other Information:

Resources:

My Maternal Great Great Great Great Great Grandmother:

Date of Birth:

Place of Birth:

Siblings:

Places of Residence:

Date of Death:

Place of Death:

Other Information:

Resources:

∞∞∞∞∞∞∞∞∞∞∞∞∞∞

My Maternal Great Great Great Great Great Grandfather:

Date of Birth:

Place of Birth:

Siblings:

Places of Residence:

Date of Death:

Place of Death:

Other Information:

Resources:

8th Generation – Son's Name:

My Maternal Great Great Great Great Great Grandmother:
Date of Birth:
Place of Birth:
Siblings:

Places of Residence:

Date of Death:
Place of Death:

Other Information:

Resources:

∞∞∞∞∞∞∞∞∞∞∞∞∞

My Maternal Great Great Great Great Great Grandfather:
Date of Birth:
Place of Birth:
Siblings:

Places of Residence:

Date of Death:
Place of Death:

Other Information:

Resources:

8th Generation – Daughter's Name:

My Maternal Great Great Great Great Great Grandmother:
Date of Birth:
Place of Birth:
Siblings:

Places of Residence:

Date of Death:
Place of Death:

Other Information:

Resources:

∞∞∞∞∞∞∞∞∞∞∞∞∞∞∞

My Maternal Great Great Great Great Great Grandfather:
Date of Birth:
Place of Birth:
Siblings:

Places of Residence:

Date of Death:
Place of Death:

Other Information:

Resources:

8th Generation – Son's Name:

My Maternal Great Great Great Great Great Grandmother:
Date of Birth:
Place of Birth:
Siblings:

Places of Residence:

Date of Death:
Place of Death:

Other Information:

Resources:

∞∞∞∞∞∞∞∞∞∞∞∞∞

My Maternal Great Great Great Great Great Grandfather:
Date of Birth:
Place of Birth:
Siblings:

Places of Residence:

Date of Death:
Place of Death:

Other Information:

Resources:

8th Generation – Daughter's Name:

My Maternal Great Great Great Great Great Grandmother:

Date of Birth:

Place of Birth:

Siblings:

Places of Residence:

Date of Death:

Place of Death:

Other Information:

Resources:

∞∞∞∞∞∞∞∞∞∞∞∞∞

My Maternal Great Great Great Great Great Grandfather:

Date of Birth:

Place of Birth:

Siblings:

Places of Residence:

Date of Death:

Place of Death:

Other Information:

Resources:

8th Generation – Son's Name:

My Maternal Great Great Great Great Great Grandmother:
Date of Birth:
Place of Birth:
Siblings:

Places of Residence:

Date of Death:
Place of Death:

Other Information:

Resources:

∞∞∞∞∞∞∞∞∞∞∞∞∞

My Maternal Great Great Great Great Great Grandfather:
Date of Birth:
Place of Birth:
Siblings:

Places of Residence:

Date of Death:
Place of Death:

Other Information:

Resources:

8th Generation – Daughter's Name:

My Maternal Great Great Great Great Great Grandmother:

Date of Birth:

Place of Birth:

Siblings:

Places of Residence:

Date of Death:

Place of Death:

Other Information:

Resources:

∞∞∞∞∞∞∞∞∞∞∞∞∞

My Maternal Great Great Great Great Great Grandfather:

Date of Birth:

Place of Birth:

Siblings:

Places of Residence:

Date of Death:

Place of Death:

Other Information:

Resources:

8th Generation – Son's Name:

My Maternal Great Great Great Great Great Grandmother:

Date of Birth:

Place of Birth:

Siblings:

Places of Residence:

Date of Death:

Place of Death:

Other Information:

Resources:

∞∞∞∞∞∞∞∞∞∞∞∞∞

My Maternal Great Great Great Great Great Grandfather:

Date of Birth:

Place of Birth:

Siblings:

Places of Residence:

Date of Death:

Place of Death:

Other Information:

Resources:

My Maternal Great Great Great Great Great Grandmother:

Date of Birth:

Place of Birth:

Siblings:

Places of Residence:

Date of Death:

Place of Death:

Other Information:

Resources:

∞∞∞∞∞∞∞∞∞∞∞∞∞

My Maternal Great Great Great Great Great Grandfather:

Date of Birth:

Place of Birth:

Siblings:

Places of Residence:

Date of Death:

Place of Death:

Other Information:

Resources:

8th Generation – Son's Name:

My Maternal Great Great Great Great Great Grandmother:
Date of Birth:
Place of Birth:
Siblings:

Places of Residence:

Date of Death:
Place of Death:

Other Information:

Resources:

∞∞∞∞∞∞∞∞∞∞∞∞∞∞

My Maternal Great Great Great Great Great Grandfather:
Date of Birth:
Place of Birth:
Siblings:

Places of Residence:

Date of Death:
Place of Death:

Other Information:

Resources:

8th Generation – Daughter's Name:

My Maternal Great Great Great Great Great Grandmother:

Date of Birth:

Place of Birth:

Siblings:

Places of Residence:

Date of Death:

Place of Death:

Other Information:

Resources:

∞∞∞∞∞∞∞∞∞∞∞∞∞∞

My Maternal Great Great Great Great Great Grandfather:

Date of Birth:

Place of Birth:

Siblings:

Places of Residence:

Date of Death:

Place of Death:

Other Information:

Resources:

8th Generation – Son's Name:

My Maternal Great Great Great Great Great Grandmother:

Date of Birth:

Place of Birth:

Siblings:

Places of Residence:

Date of Death:

Place of Death:

Other Information:

Resources:

∞∞∞∞∞∞∞∞∞∞∞∞∞

My Maternal Great Great Great Great Great Grandfather:

Date of Birth:

Place of Birth:

Siblings:

Places of Residence:

Date of Death:

Place of Death:

Other Information:

Resources:

8th Generation – Daughter's Name:

My Maternal Great Great Great Great Great Grandmother:
Date of Birth:
Place of Birth:
Siblings:

Places of Residence:

Date of Death:
Place of Death:

Other Information:

Resources:

∞∞∞∞∞∞∞∞∞∞∞∞∞∞∞

My Maternal Great Great Great Great Great Grandfather:
Date of Birth:
Place of Birth:
Siblings:

Places of Residence:

Date of Death:
Place of Death:

Other Information:

Resources:

8th Generation – Son's Name:

My Maternal Great Great Great Great Great Grandmother:
Date of Birth:
Place of Birth:
Siblings:

Places of Residence:

Date of Death:
Place of Death:

Other Information:

Resources:

∞∞∞∞∞∞∞∞∞∞∞∞∞

My Maternal Great Great Great Great Great Grandfather:
Date of Birth:
Place of Birth:
Siblings:

Places of Residence:

Date of Death:
Place of Death:

Other Information:

Resources:

My Maternal Great Great Great Great Great Grandmother:
Date of Birth:
Place of Birth:
Siblings:

Places of Residence:

Date of Death:
Place of Death:

Other Information:

Resources:

∞∞∞∞∞∞∞∞∞∞∞∞∞

My Maternal Great Great Great Great Great Grandfather:
Date of Birth:
Place of Birth:
Siblings:

Places of Residence:

Date of Death:
Place of Death:

Other Information:

Resources:

8th Generation – Son's Name:

My Maternal Great Great Great Great Great Grandmother:

Date of Birth:

Place of Birth:

Siblings:

Places of Residence:

Date of Death:

Place of Death:

Other Information:

Resources:

∞∞∞∞∞∞∞∞∞∞∞∞∞∞

My Maternal Great Great Great Great Great Grandfather:

Date of Birth:

Place of Birth:

Siblings:

Places of Residence:

Date of Death:

Place of Death:

Other Information:

Resources:

8th Generation – Daughter's Name:

My Maternal Great Great Great Great Great Grandmother:

Date of Birth:

Place of Birth:

Siblings:

Places of Residence:

Date of Death:

Place of Death:

Other Information:

Resources:

∞∞∞∞∞∞∞∞∞∞∞∞∞∞

My Maternal Great Great Great Great Great Grandfather:

Date of Birth:

Place of Birth:

Siblings:

Places of Residence:

Date of Death:

Place of Death:

Other Information:

Resources:

8th Generation – Son's Name:

My Maternal Great Great Great Great Great Grandmother:

Date of Birth:

Place of Birth:

Siblings:

Places of Residence:

Date of Death:

Place of Death:

Other Information:

Resources:

∞∞∞∞∞∞∞∞∞∞∞∞∞

My Maternal Great Great Great Great Great Grandfather:

Date of Birth:

Place of Birth:

Siblings:

Places of Residence:

Date of Death:

Place of Death:

Other Information:

Resources:

8th Generation – Daughter's Name:

My Maternal Great Great Great Great Great Grandmother:

Date of Birth:

Place of Birth:

Siblings:

Places of Residence:

Date of Death:

Place of Death:

Other Information:

Resources:

ꝏꝏꝏꝏꝏꝏꝏꝏꝏꝏꝏꝏꝏ

My Maternal Great Great Great Great Great Grandfather:

Date of Birth:

Place of Birth:

Siblings:

Places of Residence:

Date of Death:

Place of Death:

Other Information:

Resources:

My Maternal Great Great Great Great Great Grandmother:
Date of Birth:
Place of Birth:
Siblings:

Places of Residence:

Date of Death:
Place of Death:

Other Information:

Resources:

∞∞∞∞∞∞∞∞∞∞∞∞∞

My Maternal Great Great Great Great Great Grandfather:
Date of Birth:
Place of Birth:
Siblings:

Places of Residence:

Date of Death:
Place of Death:

Other Information:

Resources:

8th Generation – Daughter's Name:

My Maternal Great Great Great Great Great Grandmother:

Date of Birth:

Place of Birth:

Siblings:

Places of Residence:

Date of Death:

Place of Death:

Other Information:

Resources:

∞∞∞∞∞∞∞∞∞∞∞∞∞∞

My Maternal Great Great Great Great Great Grandfather:

Date of Birth:

Place of Birth:

Siblings:

Places of Residence:

Date of Death:

Place of Death:

Other Information:

Resources:

8th Generation – Son's Name:

My Maternal Great Great Great Great Great Grandmother:
Date of Birth:
Place of Birth:
Siblings:

Places of Residence:

Date of Death:
Place of Death:

Other Information:

Resources:

∞∞∞∞∞∞∞∞∞∞∞∞∞∞

My Maternal Great Great Great Great Great Grandfather:
Date of Birth:
Place of Birth:
Siblings:

Places of Residence:

Date of Death:
Place of Death:

Other Information:

Resources:

8th Generation – Daughter's Name:

My Maternal Great Great Great Great Great Grandmother:

Date of Birth:

Place of Birth:

Siblings:

Places of Residence:

Date of Death:

Place of Death:

Other Information:

Resources:

∞∞∞∞∞∞∞∞∞∞∞∞∞∞

My Maternal Great Great Great Great Great Grandfather:

Date of Birth:

Place of Birth:

Siblings:

Places of Residence:

Date of Death:

Place of Death:

Other Information:

Resources:

8th Generation – Son's Name:

My Maternal Great Great Great Great Great Grandmother:

Date of Birth:

Place of Birth:

Siblings:

Places of Residence:

Date of Death:

Place of Death:

Other Information:

Resources:

∞∞∞∞∞∞∞∞∞∞∞∞∞∞

My Maternal Great Great Great Great Great Grandfather:

Date of Birth:

Place of Birth:

Siblings:

Places of Residence:

Date of Death:

Place of Death:

Other Information:

Resources:

8th Generation – Daughter's Name:

My Maternal Great Great Great Great Great Grandmother:
Date of Birth:
Place of Birth:
Siblings:

Places of Residence:

Date of Death:
Place of Death:

Other Information:

Resources:

∞∞∞∞∞∞∞∞∞∞∞∞∞

My Maternal Great Great Great Great Great Grandfather:
Date of Birth:
Place of Birth:
Siblings:

Places of Residence:

Date of Death:
Place of Death:

Other Information:

Resources:

8ᵗʰ Generation – Son's Name:

My Maternal Great Great Great Great Great Grandmother:
Date of Birth:
Place of Birth:
Siblings:

Places of Residence:

Date of Death:
Place of Death:

Other Information:

Resources:

✕✕✕✕✕✕✕✕✕✕✕✕✕✕

My Maternal Great Great Great Great Great Grandfather:
Date of Birth:
Place of Birth:
Siblings:

Places of Residence:

Date of Death:
Place of Death:

Other Information:

Resources:

My Maternal Great Great Great Great Great Grandmother:
Date of Birth:
Place of Birth:
Siblings:

Places of Residence:

Date of Death:
Place of Death:

Other Information:

Resources:

∞∞∞∞∞∞∞∞∞∞∞∞∞

My Maternal Great Great Great Great Great Grandfather:
Date of Birth:
Place of Birth:
Siblings:

Places of Residence:

Date of Death:
Place of Death:

Other Information:

Resources:

My Maternal Great Great Great Great Great Grandmother:
Date of Birth:
Place of Birth:
Siblings:

Places of Residence:

Date of Death:
Place of Death:

Other Information:

Resources:

∞∞∞∞∞∞∞∞∞∞∞∞

My Maternal Great Great Great Great Great Grandfather:
Date of Birth:
Place of Birth:
Siblings:

Places of Residence:

Date of Death:
Place of Death:

Other Information:

Resources:

My Maternal Great Great Great Great Great Grandmother:
Date of Birth:
Place of Birth:
Siblings:

Places of Residence:

Date of Death:
Place of Death:

Other Information:

Resources:

∞∞∞∞∞∞∞∞∞∞∞∞∞∞

My Maternal Great Great Great Great Great Grandfather:
Date of Birth:
Place of Birth:
Siblings:

Places of Residence:

Date of Death:
Place of Death:

Other Information:

Resources:

8th Generation – Son's Name:

My Maternal Great Great Great Great Great Grandmother:

Date of Birth:

Place of Birth:

Siblings:

Places of Residence:

Date of Death:

Place of Death:

Other Information:

Resources:

∞∞∞∞∞∞∞∞∞∞∞∞∞∞

My Maternal Great Great Great Great Great Grandfather:

Date of Birth:

Place of Birth:

Siblings:

Places of Residence:

Date of Death:

Place of Death:

Other Information:

Resources:

My Maternal Great Great Great Great Great Grandmother:
Date of Birth:
Place of Birth:
Siblings:

Places of Residence:

Date of Death:
Place of Death:

Other Information:

Resources:

∞∞∞∞∞∞∞∞∞∞∞∞∞∞∞

My Maternal Great Great Great Great Great Grandfather:
Date of Birth:
Place of Birth:
Siblings:

Places of Residence:

Date of Death:
Place of Death:

Other Information:

Resources:

8th Generation – Son's Name:

My Maternal Great Great Great Great Great Grandmother:
Date of Birth:
Place of Birth:
Siblings:

Places of Residence:

Date of Death:
Place of Death:

Other Information:

Resources:

∞∞∞∞∞∞∞∞∞∞∞∞∞

My Maternal Great Great Great Great Great Grandfather:
Date of Birth:
Place of Birth:
Siblings:

Places of Residence:

Date of Death:
Place of Death:

Other Information:

Resources:

My Father's Side

2nd Generation

My Father:

Date of Birth:

Place of Birth:

Siblings:

Places of Residence:

Date of Death:

Place of Death:

Other Information:

Resources:

3rd Generation – Son's Name:

My Paternal Grandmother:

Date of Birth:

Place of Birth:

Siblings:

Places of Residence:

Date of Death:

Place of Death:

Other Information:

Resources:

∞∞∞∞∞∞∞∞∞∞∞∞∞

My Paternal Grandfather:

Date of Birth:

Place of Birth:

Siblings:

Places of Residence:

Date of Death:

Place of Death:

Other Information:

Resources:

4th Generation – Daughter's Name:

My Paternal Great Grandmother:

Date of Birth:

Place of Birth:

Siblings:

Places of Residence:

Date of Death:

Place of Death:

Other Information:

Resources:

∞∞∞∞∞∞∞∞∞∞∞∞∞

My Paternal Great Grandfather:

Date of Birth:

Place of Birth:

Siblings:

Places of Residence:

Date of Death:

Place of Death:

Other Information:

Resources:

4th Generation – Son's Name:

My Paternal Great Grandmother:
Date of Birth:
Place of Birth:
Siblings:

Places of Residence:

Date of Death:
Place of Death:

Other Information:

Resources:

∞∞∞∞∞∞∞∞∞∞∞∞∞

My Paternal Great Grandfather:
Date of Birth:
Place of Birth:
Siblings:

Places of Residence:

Date of Death:
Place of Death:

Other Information:

Resources:

5th Generation – Daughter's Name:

My Paternal Great Great Grandmother:

Date of Birth:

Place of Birth:

Siblings:

Places of Residence:

Date of Death:

Place of Death:

Other Information:

Resources:

∞∞∞∞∞∞∞∞∞∞∞∞∞∞∞

My Paternal Great Great Grandfather:

Date of Birth:

Place of Birth:

Siblings:

Places of Residence:

Date of Death:

Place of Death:

Other Information:

Resources:

5th Generation – Son's Name:

My Paternal Great Great Grandmother:

Date of Birth:

Place of Birth:

Siblings:

Places of Residence:

Date of Death:

Place of Death:

Other Information:

Resources:

∞∞∞∞∞∞∞∞∞∞∞∞

My Paternal Great Great Grandfather:

Date of Birth:

Place of Birth:

Siblings:

Places of Residence:

Date of Death:

Place of Death:

Other Information:

Resources:

My Paternal Great Great Grandmother:

Date of Birth:

Place of Birth:

Siblings:

Places of Residence:

Date of Death:

Place of Death:

Other Information:

Resources:

∞∞∞∞∞∞∞∞∞∞∞∞∞∞

My Paternal Great Great Grandfather:

Date of Birth:

Place of Birth:

Siblings:

Places of Residence:

Date of Death:

Place of Death:

Other Information:

Resources:

5th Generation – Son's Name:

My Paternal Great Great Grandmother:
Date of Birth:
Place of Birth:
Siblings:

Places of Residence:

Date of Death:
Place of Death:

Other Information:

Resources:

∞∞∞∞∞∞∞∞∞∞∞∞∞∞

My Paternal Great Great Grandfather:
Date of Birth:
Place of Birth:
Siblings:

Places of Residence:

Date of Death:
Place of Death:

Other Information:

Resources:

6th Generation – Daughter's Name:

My Paternal Great Great Great Grandmother:
Date of Birth:
Place of Birth:
Siblings:

Places of Residence:

Date of Death:
Place of Death:

Other Information:

Resources:

∞∞∞∞∞∞∞∞∞∞∞∞∞

My Paternal Great Great Great Grandfather:
Date of Birth:
Place of Birth:
Siblings:

Places of Residence:

Date of Death:
Place of Death:

Other Information:

Resources:

6th Generation – Son's Name:

My Paternal Great Great Great Grandmother:

Date of Birth:

Place of Birth:

Siblings:

Places of Residence:

Date of Death:

Place of Death:

Other Information:

Resources:

∞∞∞∞∞∞∞∞∞∞∞∞∞∞∞

My Paternal Great Great Great Grandfather:

Date of Birth:

Place of Birth:

Siblings:

Places of Residence:

Date of Death:

Place of Death:

Other Information:

Resources:

6th Generation – Daughter's Name:

My Paternal Great Great Great Grandmother:

Date of Birth:

Place of Birth:

Siblings:

Places of Residence:

Date of Death:

Place of Death:

Other Information:

Resources:

∞∞∞∞∞∞∞∞∞∞∞∞∞∞

My Paternal Great Great Great Grandfather:

Date of Birth:

Place of Birth:

Siblings:

Places of Residence:

Date of Death:

Place of Death:

Other Information:

Resources:

6th Generation – Son's Name:

My Paternal Great Great Great Grandmother:
Date of Birth:
Place of Birth:
Siblings:

Places of Residence:

Date of Death:
Place of Death:

Other Information:

Resources:

∞∞∞∞∞∞∞∞∞∞∞∞

My Paternal Great Great Great Grandfather:
Date of Birth:
Place of Birth:
Siblings:

Places of Residence:

Date of Death:
Place of Death:

Other Information:

Resources:

6th Generation – Daughter's Name:

My Paternal Great Great Great Grandmother:

Date of Birth:

Place of Birth:

Siblings:

Places of Residence:

Date of Death:

Place of Death:

Other Information:

Resources:

∞∞∞∞∞∞∞∞∞∞∞∞∞

My Paternal Great Great Great Grandfather:

Date of Birth:

Place of Birth:

Siblings:

Places of Residence:

Date of Death:

Place of Death:

Other Information:

Resources:

6th Generation – Son's Name:

My Paternal Great Great Great Grandmother:
Date of Birth:
Place of Birth:
Siblings:

Places of Residence:

Date of Death:
Place of Death:

Other Information:

Resources:

∞∞∞∞∞∞∞∞∞∞∞∞∞

My Paternal Great Great Great Grandfather:
Date of Birth:
Place of Birth:
Siblings:

Places of Residence:

Date of Death:
Place of Death:

Other Information:

Resources:

6th Generation – Daughter's Name:

My Paternal Great Great Great Grandmother:

Date of Birth:

Place of Birth:

Siblings:

Places of Residence:

Date of Death:

Place of Death:

Other Information:

Resources:

∞∞∞∞∞∞∞∞∞∞∞∞∞∞

My Paternal Great Great Great Grandfather:

Date of Birth:

Place of Birth:

Siblings:

Places of Residence:

Date of Death:

Place of Death:

Other Information:

Resources:

6th Generation – Son's Name:

My Paternal Great Great Great Grandmother:

Date of Birth:

Place of Birth:

Siblings:

Places of Residence:

Date of Death:

Place of Death:

Other Information:

Resources:

∞∞∞∞∞∞∞∞∞∞∞∞∞

My Paternal Great Great Great Grandfather:

Date of Birth:

Place of Birth:

Siblings:

Places of Residence:

Date of Death:

Place of Death:

Other Information:

Resources:

My Paternal Great Great Great Great Grandmother:

Date of Birth:

Place of Birth:

Siblings:

Places of Residence:

Date of Death:

Place of Death:

Other Information:

Resources:

∞∞∞∞∞∞∞∞∞∞∞∞∞∞∞

My Paternal Great Great Great Great Grandfather:

Date of Birth:

Place of Birth:

Siblings:

Places of Residence:

Date of Death:

Place of Death:

Other Information:

Resources:

My Paternal Great Great Great Great Grandmother:

Date of Birth:

Place of Birth:

Siblings:

Places of Residence:

Date of Death:

Place of Death:

Other Information:

Resources:

∞∞∞∞∞∞∞∞∞∞∞∞∞

My Paternal Great Great Great Great Grandfather:

Date of Birth:

Place of Birth:

Siblings:

Places of Residence:

Date of Death:

Place of Death:

Other Information:

Resources:

My Paternal Great Great Great Great Grandmother:
Date of Birth:
Place of Birth:
Siblings:

Places of Residence:

Date of Death:
Place of Death:

Other Information:

Resources:

ထထထထထထထထထထထထ

My Paternal Great Great Great Great Grandfather:
Date of Birth:
Place of Birth:
Siblings:

Places of Residence:

Date of Death:
Place of Death:

Other Information:

Resources:

7th Generation – Son's Name:

My Paternal Great Great Great Great Grandmother:

Date of Birth:

Place of Birth:

Siblings:

Places of Residence:

Date of Death:

Place of Death:

Other Information:

Resources:

∞∞∞∞∞∞∞∞∞∞∞∞∞∞

My Paternal Great Great Great Great Grandfather:

Date of Birth:

Place of Birth:

Siblings:

Places of Residence:

Date of Death:

Place of Death:

Other Information:

Resources:

My Paternal Great Great Great Great Grandmother:

Date of Birth:

Place of Birth:

Siblings:

Places of Residence:

Date of Death:

Place of Death:

Other Information:

Resources:

∞∞∞∞∞∞∞∞∞∞∞∞∞∞

My Paternal Great Great Great Great Grandfather:

Date of Birth:

Place of Birth:

Siblings:

Places of Residence:

Date of Death:

Place of Death:

Other Information:

Resources:

7ᵗʰ Generation – Son's Name:

My Paternal Great Great Great Great Grandmother:
Date of Birth:
Place of Birth:
Siblings:

Places of Residence:

Date of Death:
Place of Death:

Other Information:

Resources:

∞∞∞∞∞∞∞∞∞∞∞∞∞

My Paternal Great Great Great Great Grandfather:
Date of Birth:
Place of Birth:
Siblings:

Places of Residence:

Date of Death:
Place of Death:

Other Information:

Resources:

7th Generation – Daughter's Name:

My Paternal Great Great Great Great Grandmother:

Date of Birth:

Place of Birth:

Siblings:

Places of Residence:

Date of Death:

Place of Death:

Other Information:

Resources:

⦾⦾⦾⦾⦾⦾⦾⦾⦾⦾⦾⦾⦾⦾⦾

My Paternal Great Great Great Great Grandfather:

Date of Birth:

Place of Birth:

Siblings:

Places of Residence:

Date of Death:

Place of Death:

Other Information:

Resources:

My Paternal Great Great Great Great Grandmother:

Date of Birth:

Place of Birth:

Siblings:

Places of Residence:

Date of Death:

Place of Death:

Other Information:

Resources:

∞∞∞∞∞∞∞∞∞∞∞∞∞

My Paternal Great Great Great Great Grandfather:

Date of Birth:

Place of Birth:

Siblings:

Places of Residence:

Date of Death:

Place of Death:

Other Information:

Resources:

My Paternal Great Great Great Great Grandmother:
Date of Birth:
Place of Birth:
Siblings:

Places of Residence:

Date of Death:
Place of Death:

Other Information:

Resources:

∞∞∞∞∞∞∞∞∞∞∞∞∞∞

My Paternal Great Great Great Great Grandfather:
Date of Birth:
Place of Birth:
Siblings:

Places of Residence:

Date of Death:
Place of Death:

Other Information:

Resources:

7th Generation – Son's Name:

My Paternal Great Great Great Great Grandmother:

Date of Birth:

Place of Birth:

Siblings:

Places of Residence:

Date of Death:

Place of Death:

Other Information:

Resources:

∞∞∞∞∞∞∞∞∞∞∞∞∞

My Paternal Great Great Great Great Grandfather:

Date of Birth:

Place of Birth:

Siblings:

Places of Residence:

Date of Death:

Place of Death:

Other Information:

Resources:

My Paternal Great Great Great Great Grandmother:
Date of Birth:
Place of Birth:
Siblings:

Places of Residence:

Date of Death:
Place of Death:

Other Information:

Resources:

∞∞∞∞∞∞∞∞∞∞∞∞∞

My Paternal Great Great Great Great Grandfather:
Date of Birth:
Place of Birth:
Siblings:

Places of Residence:

Date of Death:
Place of Death:

Other Information:

Resources:

7th Generation – Son's Name:

My Paternal Great Great Great Great Grandmother:
Date of Birth:
Place of Birth:
Siblings:

Places of Residence:

Date of Death:
Place of Death:

Other Information:

Resources:

∞∞∞∞∞∞∞∞∞∞∞∞∞

My Paternal Great Great Great Great Grandfather:
Date of Birth:
Place of Birth:
Siblings:

Places of Residence:

Date of Death:
Place of Death:

Other Information:

Resources:

My Paternal Great Great Great Great Grandmother:

Date of Birth:

Place of Birth:

Siblings:

Places of Residence:

Date of Death:

Place of Death:

Other Information:

Resources:

∞∞∞∞∞∞∞∞∞∞∞∞∞

My Paternal Great Great Great Great Grandfather:

Date of Birth:

Place of Birth:

Siblings:

Places of Residence:

Date of Death:

Place of Death:

Other Information:

Resources:

7th Generation – Son's Name:

My Paternal Great Great Great Great Grandmother:
Date of Birth:
Place of Birth:
Siblings:

Places of Residence:

Date of Death:
Place of Death:

Other Information:

Resources:

∞∞∞∞∞∞∞∞∞∞∞∞∞

My Paternal Great Great Great Great Grandfather:
Date of Birth:
Place of Birth:
Siblings:

Places of Residence:

Date of Death:
Place of Death:

Other Information:

Resources:

7th Generation – Daughter's Name:

My Paternal Great Great Great Great Grandmother:

Date of Birth:

Place of Birth:

Siblings:

Places of Residence:

Date of Death:

Place of Death:

Other Information:

Resources:

∞∞∞∞∞∞∞∞∞∞∞∞∞∞

My Paternal Great Great Great Great Grandfather:

Date of Birth:

Place of Birth:

Siblings:

Places of Residence:

Date of Death:

Place of Death:

Other Information:

Resources:

7th Generation – Son's Name:

My Paternal Great Great Great Great Grandmother:

Date of Birth:

Place of Birth:

Siblings:

Places of Residence:

Date of Death:

Place of Death:

Other Information:

Resources:

∞∞∞∞∞∞∞∞∞∞∞∞∞

My Paternal Great Great Great Great Grandfather:

Date of Birth:

Place of Birth:

Siblings:

Places of Residence:

Date of Death:

Place of Death:

Other Information:

Resources:

My Paternal Great Great Great Great Great Grandmother:

Date of Birth:

Place of Birth:

Siblings:

Places of Residence:

Date of Death:

Place of Death:

Other Information:

Resources:

ᏅᏅᏅᏅᏅᏅᏅᏅᏅᏅᏅᏅᏅᏅ

My Paternal Great Great Great Great Great Grandfather:

Date of Birth:

Place of Birth:

Siblings:

Places of Residence:

Date of Death:

Place of Death:

Other Information:

Resources:

My Paternal Great Great Great Great Great Grandmother:

Date of Birth:

Place of Birth:

Siblings:

Places of Residence:

Date of Death:

Place of Death:

Other Information:

Resources:

∞∞∞∞∞∞∞∞∞∞∞∞∞∞∞

My Paternal Great Great Great Great Great Grandfather:

Date of Birth:

Place of Birth:

Siblings:

Places of Residence:

Date of Death:

Place of Death:

Other Information:

Resources:

8th Generation – Daughter's Name:

My Paternal Great Great Great Great Great Grandmother:

Date of Birth:

Place of Birth:

Siblings:

Places of Residence:

Date of Death:

Place of Death:

Other Information:

Resources:

∞∞∞∞∞∞∞∞∞∞∞∞∞∞

My Paternal Great Great Great Great Great Grandfather:

Date of Birth:

Place of Birth:

Siblings:

Places of Residence:

Date of Death:

Place of Death:

Other Information:

Resources:

My Paternal Great Great Great Great Great Grandmother:

Date of Birth:

Place of Birth:

Siblings:

Places of Residence:

Date of Death:

Place of Death:

Other Information:

Resources:

∞∞∞∞∞∞∞∞∞∞∞∞∞∞

My Paternal Great Great Great Great Great Grandfather:

Date of Birth:

Place of Birth:

Siblings:

Places of Residence:

Date of Death:

Place of Death:

Other Information:

Resources:

8th Generation – Daughter's Name:

My Paternal Great Great Great Great Great Grandmother:

Date of Birth:

Place of Birth:

Siblings:

Places of Residence:

Date of Death:

Place of Death:

Other Information:

Resources:

∞∞∞∞∞∞∞∞∞∞∞∞∞∞∞

My Paternal Great Great Great Great Great Grandfather:

Date of Birth:

Place of Birth:

Siblings:

Places of Residence:

Date of Death:

Place of Death:

Other Information:

Resources:

8th Generation – Son's Name:

My Paternal Great Great Great Great Great Grandmother:

Date of Birth:

Place of Birth:

Siblings:

Places of Residence:

Date of Death:

Place of Death:

Other Information:

Resources:

∞∞∞∞∞∞∞∞∞∞∞∞∞

My Paternal Great Great Great Great Great Grandfather:

Date of Birth:

Place of Birth:

Siblings:

Places of Residence:

Date of Death:

Place of Death:

Other Information:

Resources:

8th Generation – Daughter's Name:

My Paternal Great Great Great Great Great Grandmother:
Date of Birth:
Place of Birth:
Siblings:

Places of Residence:

Date of Death:
Place of Death:

Other Information:

Resources:

⦾⦾⦾⦾⦾⦾⦾⦾⦾⦾⦾⦾⦾⦾⦾

My Paternal Great Great Great Great Great Grandfather:
Date of Birth:
Place of Birth:
Siblings:

Places of Residence:

Date of Death:
Place of Death:

Other Information:

Resources:

8th Generation – Son's Name:

My Paternal Great Great Great Great Great Grandmother:

Date of Birth:

Place of Birth:

Siblings:

Places of Residence:

Date of Death:

Place of Death:

Other Information:

Resources:

∞∞∞∞∞∞∞∞∞∞∞∞∞∞

My Paternal Great Great Great Great Great Grandfather:

Date of Birth:

Place of Birth:

Siblings:

Places of Residence:

Date of Death:

Place of Death:

Other Information:

Resources:

My Paternal Great Great Great Great Great Grandmother:

Date of Birth:

Place of Birth:

Siblings:

Places of Residence:

Date of Death:

Place of Death:

Other Information:

Resources:

∞∞∞∞∞∞∞∞∞∞∞∞∞

My Paternal Great Great Great Great Great Grandfather:

Date of Birth:

Place of Birth:

Siblings:

Places of Residence:

Date of Death:

Place of Death:

Other Information:

Resources:

My Paternal Great Great Great Great Great Grandmother:

Date of Birth:

Place of Birth:

Siblings:

Places of Residence:

Date of Death:

Place of Death:

Other Information:

Resources:

∞∞∞∞∞∞∞∞∞∞∞∞∞

My Paternal Great Great Great Great Great Grandfather:

Date of Birth:

Place of Birth:

Siblings:

Places of Residence:

Date of Death:

Place of Death:

Other Information:

Resources:

8th Generation – Daughter's Name:

My Paternal Great Great Great Great Great Grandmother:

Date of Birth:

Place of Birth:

Siblings:

Places of Residence:

Date of Death:

Place of Death:

Other Information:

Resources:

∞∞∞∞∞∞∞∞∞∞∞∞∞∞

My Paternal Great Great Great Great Great Grandfather:

Date of Birth:

Place of Birth:

Siblings:

Places of Residence:

Date of Death:

Place of Death:

Other Information:

Resources:

8th Generation – Son's Name:

My Paternal Great Great Great Great Great Grandmother:
Date of Birth:
Place of Birth:
Siblings:

Places of Residence:

Date of Death:
Place of Death:

Other Information:

Resources:

∞∞∞∞∞∞∞∞∞∞∞∞∞

My Paternal Great Great Great Great Great Grandfather:
Date of Birth:
Place of Birth:
Siblings:

Places of Residence:

Date of Death:
Place of Death:

Other Information:

Resources:

My Paternal Great Great Great Great Great Grandmother:

Date of Birth:

Place of Birth:

Siblings:

Places of Residence:

Date of Death:

Place of Death:

Other Information:

Resources:

∞∞∞∞∞∞∞∞∞∞∞∞∞

My Paternal Great Great Great Great Great Grandfather:

Date of Birth:

Place of Birth:

Siblings:

Places of Residence:

Date of Death:

Place of Death:

Other Information:

Resources:

8th Generation – Son's Name:

My Paternal Great Great Great Great Great Grandmother:

Date of Birth:

Place of Birth:

Siblings:

Places of Residence:

Date of Death:

Place of Death:

Other Information:

Resources:

∞∞∞∞∞∞∞∞∞∞∞∞∞

My Paternal Great Great Great Great Great Grandfather:

Date of Birth:

Place of Birth:

Siblings:

Places of Residence:

Date of Death:

Place of Death:

Other Information:

Resources:

My Paternal Great Great Great Great Great Grandmother:

Date of Birth:

Place of Birth:

Siblings:

Places of Residence:

Date of Death:

Place of Death:

Other Information:

Resources:

∞∞∞∞∞∞∞∞∞∞∞∞∞

My Paternal Great Great Great Great Great Grandfather:

Date of Birth:

Place of Birth:

Siblings:

Places of Residence:

Date of Death:

Place of Death:

Other Information:

Resources:

8th Generation – Son's Name:

My Paternal Great Great Great Great Great Grandmother:

Date of Birth:

Place of Birth:

Siblings:

Places of Residence:

Date of Death:

Place of Death:

Other Information:

Resources:

∞∞∞∞∞∞∞∞∞∞∞∞∞

My Paternal Great Great Great Great Great Grandfather:

Date of Birth:

Place of Birth:

Siblings:

Places of Residence:

Date of Death:

Place of Death:

Other Information:

Resources:

My Paternal Great Great Great Great Great Grandmother:

Date of Birth:

Place of Birth:

Siblings:

Places of Residence:

Date of Death:

Place of Death:

Other Information:

Resources:

∞∞∞∞∞∞∞∞∞∞∞∞∞∞

My Paternal Great Great Great Great Great Grandfather:

Date of Birth:

Place of Birth:

Siblings:

Places of Residence:

Date of Death:

Place of Death:

Other Information:

Resources:

8th Generation – Son's Name:

My Paternal Great Great Great Great Great Grandmother:

Date of Birth:

Place of Birth:

Siblings:

Places of Residence:

Date of Death:

Place of Death:

Other Information:

Resources:

∞∞∞∞∞∞∞∞∞∞∞∞∞∞

My Paternal Great Great Great Great Great Grandfather:

Date of Birth:

Place of Birth:

Siblings:

Places of Residence:

Date of Death:

Place of Death:

Other Information:

Resources:

8ᵗʰ Generation – Daughter's Name:

My Paternal Great Great Great Great Great Grandmother:

Date of Birth:

Place of Birth:

Siblings:

Places of Residence:

Date of Death:

Place of Death:

Other Information:

Resources:

∞∞∞∞∞∞∞∞∞∞∞∞∞

My Paternal Great Great Great Great Great Grandfather:

Date of Birth:

Place of Birth:

Siblings:

Places of Residence:

Date of Death:

Place of Death:

Other Information:

Resources:

8th Generation – Son's Name:

My Paternal Great Great Great Great Great Grandmother:

Date of Birth:

Place of Birth:

Siblings:

Places of Residence:

Date of Death:

Place of Death:

Other Information:

Resources:

∞∞∞∞∞∞∞∞∞∞∞∞

My Paternal Great Great Great Great Great Grandfather:

Date of Birth:

Place of Birth:

Siblings:

Places of Residence:

Date of Death:

Place of Death:

Other Information:

Resources:

My Paternal Great Great Great Great Great Grandmother:

Date of Birth:

Place of Birth:

Siblings:

Places of Residence:

Date of Death:

Place of Death:

Other Information:

Resources:

❁❁❁❁❁❁❁❁❁❁❁❁❁❁

My Paternal Great Great Great Great Great Grandfather:

Date of Birth:

Place of Birth:

Siblings:

Places of Residence:

Date of Death:

Place of Death:

Other Information:

Resources:

8ᵗʰ Generation – Son's Name:

My Paternal Great Great Great Great Great Grandmother:

Date of Birth:

Place of Birth:

Siblings:

Places of Residence:

Date of Death:

Place of Death:

Other Information:

Resources:

∞∞∞∞∞∞∞∞∞∞∞∞∞

My Paternal Great Great Great Great Great Grandfather:

Date of Birth:

Place of Birth:

Siblings:

Places of Residence:

Date of Death:

Place of Death:

Other Information:

Resources:

8th Generation – Daughter's Name:

My Paternal Great Great Great Great Great Grandmother:

Date of Birth:

Place of Birth:

Siblings:

Places of Residence:

Date of Death:

Place of Death:

Other Information:

Resources:

∞∞∞∞∞∞∞∞∞∞∞∞∞

My Paternal Great Great Great Great Great Grandfather:

Date of Birth:

Place of Birth:

Siblings:

Places of Residence:

Date of Death:

Place of Death:

Other Information:

Resources:

My Paternal Great Great Great Great Great Grandmother:

Date of Birth:

Place of Birth:

Siblings:

Places of Residence:

Date of Death:

Place of Death:

Other Information:

Resources:

∞∞∞∞∞∞∞∞∞∞∞∞∞∞∞

My Paternal Great Great Great Great Great Grandfather:

Date of Birth:

Place of Birth:

Siblings:

Places of Residence:

Date of Death:

Place of Death:

Other Information:

Resources:

My Paternal Great Great Great Great Great Grandmother:

Date of Birth:

Place of Birth:

Siblings:

Places of Residence:

Date of Death:

Place of Death:

Other Information:

Resources:

∞∞∞∞∞∞∞∞∞∞∞∞∞

My Paternal Great Great Great Great Great Grandfather:

Date of Birth:

Place of Birth:

Siblings:

Places of Residence:

Date of Death:

Place of Death:

Other Information:

Resources:

8th Generation – Son's Name:

My Paternal Great Great Great Great Great Grandmother:

Date of Birth:

Place of Birth:

Siblings:

Places of Residence:

Date of Death:

Place of Death:

Other Information:

Resources:

∞∞∞∞∞∞∞∞∞∞∞∞∞∞

My Paternal Great Great Great Great Great Grandfather:

Date of Birth:

Place of Birth:

Siblings:

Places of Residence:

Date of Death:

Place of Death:

Other Information:

Resources:

8th Generation – Daughter's Name:

My Paternal Great Great Great Great Great Grandmother:

Date of Birth:

Place of Birth:

Siblings:

Places of Residence:

Date of Death:

Place of Death:

Other Information:

Resources:

∞∞∞∞∞∞∞∞∞∞∞∞∞

My Paternal Great Great Great Great Great Grandfather:

Date of Birth:

Place of Birth:

Siblings:

Places of Residence:

Date of Death:

Place of Death:

Other Information:

Resources:

My Paternal Great Great Great Great Great Grandmother:

Date of Birth:

Place of Birth:

Siblings:

Places of Residence:

Date of Death:

Place of Death:

Other Information:

Resources:

∞∞∞∞∞∞∞∞∞∞∞∞∞∞∞

My Paternal Great Great Great Great Great Grandfather:

Date of Birth:

Place of Birth:

Siblings:

Places of Residence:

Date of Death:

Place of Death:

Other Information:

Resources:

8th Generation – Daughter's Name:

My Paternal Great Great Great Great Great Grandmother:

Date of Birth:

Place of Birth:

Siblings:

Places of Residence:

Date of Death:

Place of Death:

Other Information:

Resources:

∞∞∞∞∞∞∞∞∞∞∞∞∞∞∞

My Paternal Great Great Great Great Great Grandfather:

Date of Birth:

Place of Birth:

Siblings:

Places of Residence:

Date of Death:

Place of Death:

Other Information:

Resources:

8th Generation – Son's Name:

My Paternal Great Great Great Great Great Grandmother:
Date of Birth:
Place of Birth:
Siblings:

Places of Residence:

Date of Death:
Place of Death:

Other Information:

Resources:

∞∞∞∞∞∞∞∞∞∞∞∞∞

My Paternal Great Great Great Great Great Grandfather:
Date of Birth:
Place of Birth:
Siblings:

Places of Residence:

Date of Death:
Place of Death:

Other Information:

Resources:

My Paternal Great Great Great Great Great Grandmother:
Date of Birth:
Place of Birth:
Siblings:

Places of Residence:

Date of Death:
Place of Death:

Other Information:

Resources:

∞∞∞∞∞∞∞∞∞∞∞∞∞∞∞

My Paternal Great Great Great Great Great Grandfather:
Date of Birth:
Place of Birth:
Siblings:

Places of Residence:

Date of Death:
Place of Death:

Other Information:

Resources:

8th Generation – Son's Name:

My Paternal Great Great Great Great Great Grandmother:

Date of Birth:

Place of Birth:

Siblings:

Places of Residence:

Date of Death:

Place of Death:

Other Information:

Resources:

∞∞∞∞∞∞∞∞∞∞∞∞∞∞∞

My Paternal Great Great Great Great Great Grandfather:

Date of Birth:

Place of Birth:

Siblings:

Places of Residence:

Date of Death:

Place of Death:

Other Information:

Resources:

Made in the USA
Lexington, KY
28 November 2018